I0018037

How to Create a Vivid Town

Town

in Clip Studio Paint

How to Create a Vivid Town

in Clip Studio Paint

-

A Creative Journey in Digital Painting

Grandpa Edo

Copyright © 2024 Grandpa Edo

All rights reserved.

ISBN: 9798329064049

Imprint: Independently published

DEDICATION

This book is dedicated to my family, friends and all the people who ever supported me. Thank you!

CONTENTS

ACKNOWLEDGMENTS

This book serves the purposes of education, entertainment, and inspiration.

Grandpa Edo, the author of this mini book and the artist behind the digital painting featured herein, has no affiliation with the software developer "Celsys", creator of "Clip Studio".

The rights to the Clip Studio Assets utilized within this mini book belong to their respective original creators.

INTRODUCTION

Welcome to this tutorial, where I will take you through my creative journey and offer tips on crafting a vibrant small town. This is more than a digital painting tutorial; it is meant to inspire you to imagine.

While I use Clip Studio Paint for this demonstration, you can apply the techniques with similar software or draw inspiration for your conceptual projects. Please remember that the creative process matters more than any specific software.

This step-by-step walkthrough is divided into three chapters:

Chapter 1 – You Are an Architect

- Perspective drawing
- Utilizing perspective rulers in Clip Studio Paint
- Creating initial line art of the small town
- Adding characters using 2D methods within the perspective view
- Adding characters using 3D methods within the perspective view

Chapter 2 – You Are God

- Coloring techniques
- Incorporating sky and clouds 1 – creating custom clouds
- Incorporating sky and clouds 2 - importing image material
- Adding various plants 1 – crafting your own plants
- Adding various plants 2 – using brushes for plant creation
- Including other small objects like bicycles and footballs using the 3D method

Chapter 3 – You Are a Director

- Telling a story through staging extras
- Adding texture to enhance realism
- Incorporating shadows for depth
- Including small details to enrich the scene

Let's jump into this creative adventure together!

Creativity is an imaginative journey.

Grandpa Edo

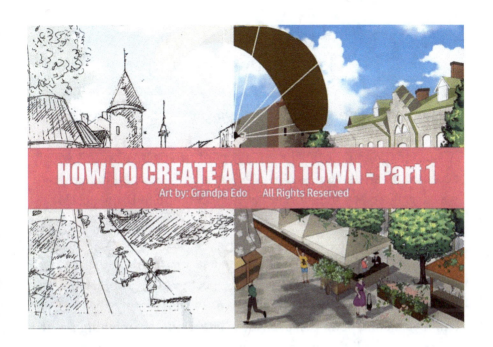

Art by: Grandpa Edo   All Rights Reserved

CHAPTER 1

You Are an Architect

Creating art is not a linear journey. When it comes to drawing or concept art, I often begin with a hand-drawn sketch to capture an organic essence. From there, I transition to digital mediums.

For this project, my inspiration came from a quaint town featuring a medieval-style castle. Starting with a hand-drawn sketch allows me to observe the object and immerse myself in the location's atmosphere.

Perspective Drawing

At this stage, you are essentially playing the role of an Architect.

It's fascinating to note that the concept of perspective wasn't widely accepted by artists until the late 15th century. The revolutionary rule was discovered by the Florentine Architect Filippo Brunelleschi during the early Renaissance period.

Perspective is all about creating depth and space within the 2D dimension. A fundamental rule of perspective is that **objects appear larger the closer they are to us, the observers**. In my sketch, I've employed a one-point perspective, where a **single vanishing point** (marked by the little red dot) sits on the horizon line (depicted by the blue line). All parallel lines within the scene converge towards this little red dot – a vanishing point, as its name suggests.

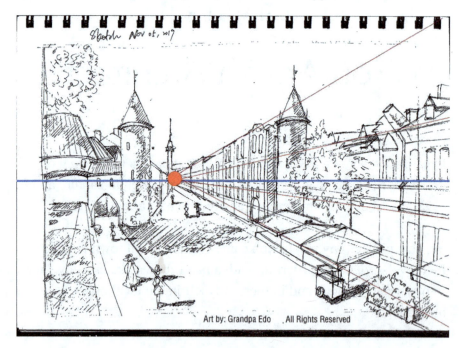

Art by: Grandpa Edo   . All Rights Reserved

Perspective Rulers in Clip Studio Paint

Now, let's bring my sketch into Clip Studio Paint (or any similar software). I've opted for an Illustration template, with a canvas size of 4565 pixels (width) by 3096 pixels (height) and a resolution of 300.

To import the sketch, simply navigate to **File** > **Import** > **Image**. Once imported, you will find the sketch within Clip Studio Paint.

Next, I'll adjust the opacity of the sketch to 30%.

This sets the stage for applying the perspective ruler.

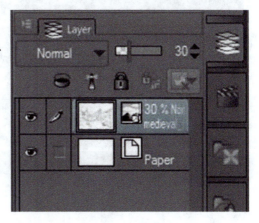

Then, click Layer > Ruler – Frame > Create Perspective Ruler.

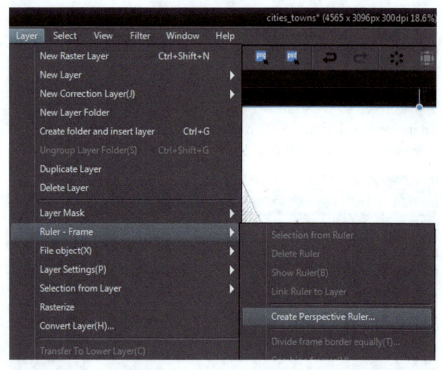

A pop-up screen will appear asking you to choose the perspective type. Simply click "1 point perspective".

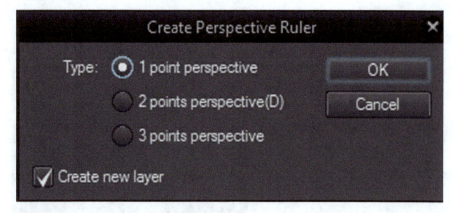

The one-point perspective ruler will then appear on your canvas, and you will have a separate layer for the perspective ruler automatically created.

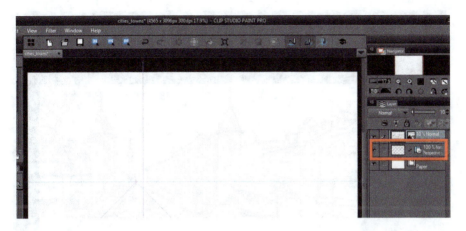

Now click the "**Operation**" icon to play around with this perspective ruler. You can adjust the height of the horizon (eye level) by clicking the "converging point" – our **Vanishing Point** (which will turn **RED** after clicking) -- or drag the Vanishing Point horizontally to locate the ideal position.

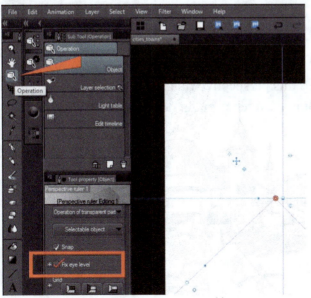

Once you are happy with the eye level's height, you can select "**Fix eye level**", and the eye level's height will be locked in place.

Likewise, feel free to experiment with the other guidelines to assess the angle of your perspective ruler.

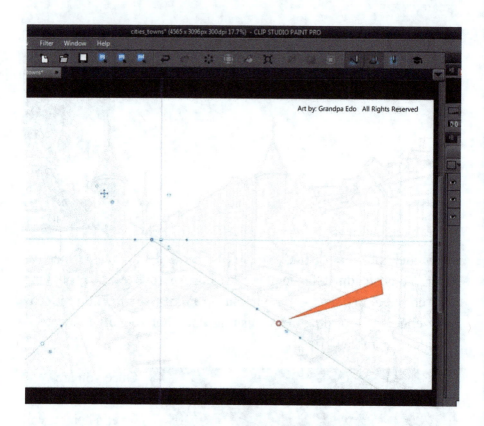

In my case, I utilized this perspective ruler to align with my original sketch since hand-drawn sketches might not accurately capture perspective.

Initial Line Art of Small Town

For the initial line art of this artwork, I would like to see a clean, almost mechanical style, akin to an engineer's draft.

To achieve this, I set the "**Line**" tool - > "**Straight line**" with a brush size of 1.0 pixel to meticulously trace my sketch.

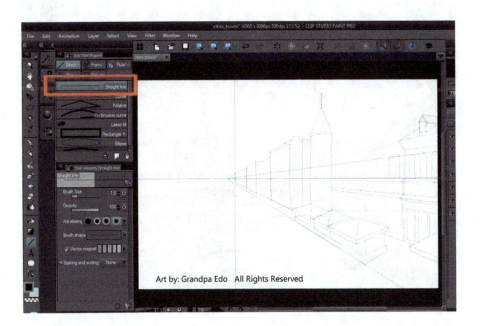

Art by: Grandpa Edo   All Rights Reserved

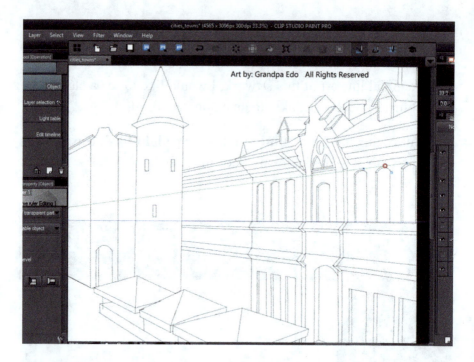

We now have a crisp, precise outline of the buildings. To complete the scene, I'll add one more thing - **characters**, and then we will be ready for the coloring stage.

Adding 2D Characters in the Perspective

A small town without characters will be quite boring. To inject life into our small-town scene, let's introduce some characters! We have the option to depict them in either 2D or 3D style. For starters, let's invite a flying doctor from the Edo Period to pay a visit to this small town (This flying doctor is my original creation).

To incorporate the line art of the flying doctor into our scene, we'll navigate to **File > Import > Image**.

The image will be imported automatically in vector format.

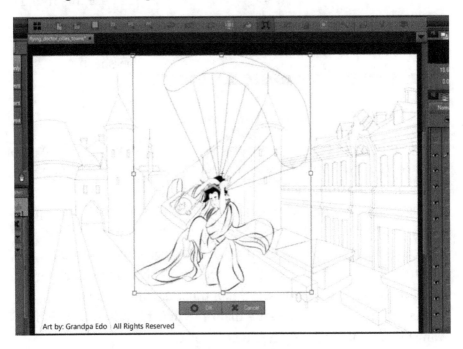

Art by: Grandpa Edo | All Rights Reserved

One thing we must bear in mind is that the character's perspective view should match the perspective of the small town. With this pose, the perspective doesn't need to be very complicated. We can use this flying doctor's medical box to test the perspective.

Art by: Grandpa Edo   All Rights Reserved

Three-point perspective – this perspective comes into play here because she is flying in the sky, introducing another vanishing point: the **height vanishing point.** This additional point is typically represented in a three-point perspective. The fundamental principle of this perspective is that when the object is **below our eye level** (in this case, we are looking down), the height vanishing point is positioned below the object. In our scenario, the height vanishing point lies outside the canvas. We can illustrate this in the next screenshot of the final line art – that **blue point** denotes the height vanishing point for the flying doctor's box.

Art by: Grandpa Edo   All Rights Reserved

Adding 3D Characters in the Perspective

Next, let's explore Clip Studio Paint's asset warehouse to import a 3D model onto the canvas.

To access the assets, navigate to **Window** > **Material** > **Material [Material]**.

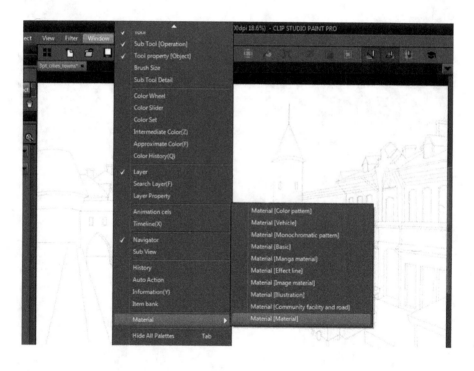

From there, click on **3D > Pose > Entire body**, where you'll find an array of 3D models to choose from.

Simply select the model you prefer and drag and drop it directly onto the canvas.

I finally opted for this particular pose as it seems fitting for my scene. Once the 3D model is on the canvas, you will notice small icons, known as **control handles**, above the model. These can be manipulated to adjust the position and orientation of the model to suit your needs.

To customize the lighting for the desired effect, click the "+" icon next to "Apply light source" on the left panel labeled "3D drawing figure editing". Use the control ball to rotate and position the light source accordingly. In my hand-drawn sketch, the shadow falls on the right-hand side, so we need to adjust the lighting to match.

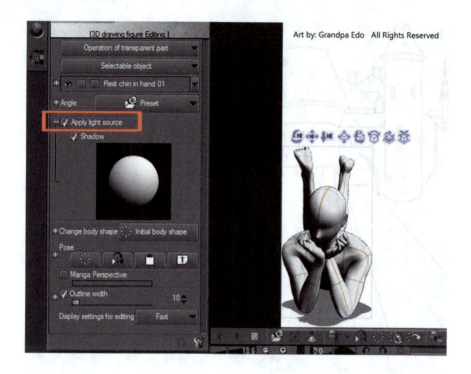

Art by: Grandpa Edo   All Rights Reserved

Next, click the "+" icon next to the "**Angle**" button to open the control panel for **Camera Perspective**. Experiment with the sliders for Perspective, Roll and Camera Position (X, Y, Z) to achieve your desired perspective and angle. In my scene, the 3D model is positioned beside a large lawn, elevated above the pedestrian pathway. Therefore, her position should be **lower than** the flying doctor's box, but **higher than** the other people on the ground (whom we will add later).

If this 3D model is positioned lower than the flying doctor's box, we should be looking down at her. Consequently, we can see a larger portion of her skullcap. Additionally, given her lying position, we need to consider the basic principle of perspective – the closer an object is, the larger it appears.

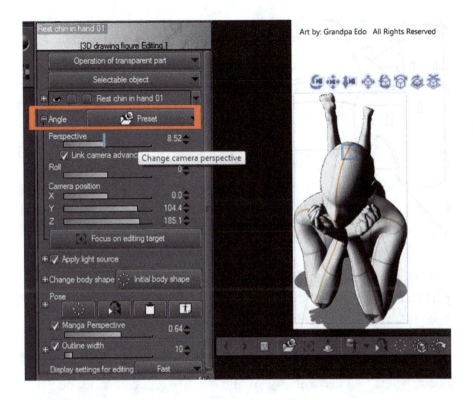

Art by: Grandpa Edo   All Rights Reserved

As a result, her feet should appear much smaller to convey perspective accurately. Use the control icons above her head to fine-tune her perspective.

This process is enjoyable and intuitive, allowing for creative experimentation.

After rasterizing the 3D model layer and scaling it down to a smaller size, I proceed to trace the outline of the model to give her a more natural appearance, as if she were lying there and listening to music.

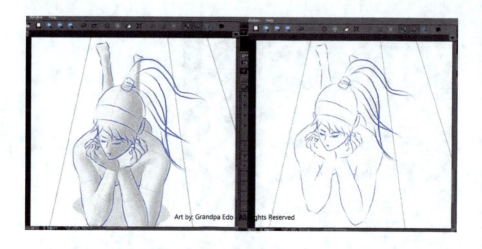

Art by: Grandpa Edo All Rights Reserved

This step allows us to address the issue of **"foreshortening"**, particularly with the flying doctor's left foot. Foreshortening becomes apparent when viewing the character from a perspective angle. Adhering to the golden rule of perspective – **where the closer an object is, the larger it appears** – we adjust the size of the flying doctor's left foot accordingly. While the difference may not be dramatic in this scene, it helps maintain visual coherence.

Art by: Grandpa Edo   All Rights Reserved

With the small town, the flying doctor, and our additional character in place, it's understandable if your're feeling fatigued by the strict adherence to perspective principles. Perhaps it's time to step away from the role of an architect and embrace a more God-like approach as we transition to the next stage of our creation – You are God!

Art by: Grandpa Edo   All Rights Reserved

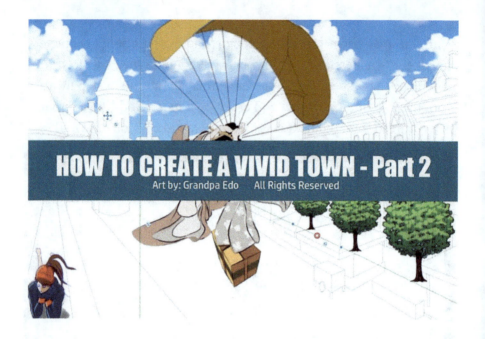

Art by: Grandpa Edo   All Rights Reserved

CHAPTER 2

You Are God

God is widely recognized as a great Creator and Painter, a notion with which few would argue. In Part 2, our task is to unveil the beauty of Mother Nature within our small town. We'll breathe life into this virtual world by infusing it with colors and other essential components.

Coloring Techniques

There is a wonderfully intuitive and relaxed method for coloring artwork in Clip Studio Paint that only requires a single step.

Simply click the "**Fill**" icon, point to the areas where you want to apply the same color, and then drag to paint all at once. This process automatically fills your desired areas with the same color, eliminating the need to use "Auto Select" followed by "Fill". It works seamlessly, much like any brush or pen tool. Just remember to ensure that the "**Close gap**" option is enabled, conveniently located on the left panel.

Art by: Grandpa Edo All Rights Reserved

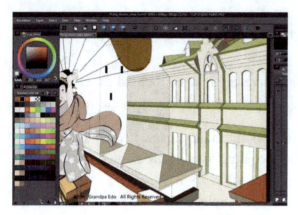

With this method, you can quickly fill colors for both characters and buildings.

Adding Sky & Cloud 1 –

Creating Custom Clouds

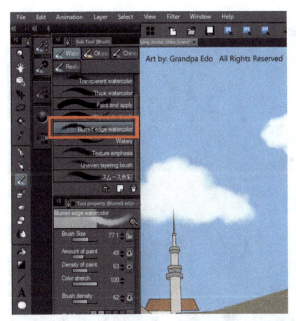

Art by: Grandpa Edo   All Rights Reserved

Now, we can proceed to add the sky and clouds. To paint the clouds, I use **Brush > Watercolor > Blurred edge watercolor**. By adjusting the values of the Amount of paint, Density of paint, and Brush density, you can achieve your desired effect.

With the base of the sky and clouds established, if you're satisfied with it and have the time, you can further enhance the realism by painting detailed clouds and sky. However, since this isn't the primary focus of the tutorial, let's explore a faster shortcut to achieve our desired outcome.

Art by: Grandpa Edo   All Rights Reserved

Adding Sky & Cloud 2 –

Importing Image Material

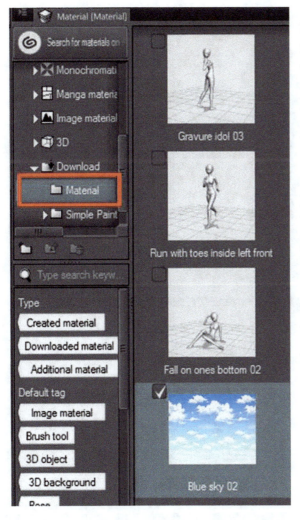

Sometimes, we don't need to reinvent the wheel, and that's when we might want to explore the Material Library.

Navigate to **Window** > **Material** > **Material [Material],** then select **Download** > **Material**. Here, you'll find the Blue Sky 02 image material.

Simply drag and drop it onto the canvas. The scene now takes on a surreal appearance. You might want to fine-tune the image, perhaps adjusting the position of the clouds, just to ensure it meets your satisfaction.

Art by: Grandpa Edo   All Rights Reserved

Now let's create a Layer Mask for our sky.

1. First, **de-select** the layer of the Blue-Sky Image.

2. Navigate to the **line art layer** or **the layer with a solid color representing the sky.** Use the **Auto Select tool** to select the outline of the sky. Ensure that you have a closed skyline for accurate selection.

3. With the outline of the sky selected, return to selecting the Blue-Sky Image Material layer AGAIN.

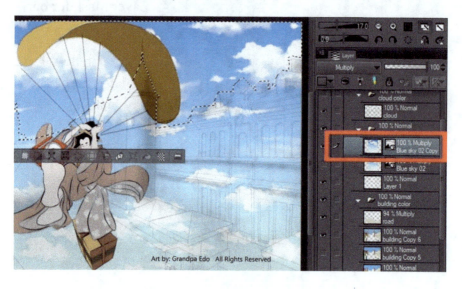

4. Right-click the Blue-Sky Image Material layer and select **Layer Mask > Mask Outside Selection (V)**.

Voila! The sky mask is complete!

Art by: Grandpa Edo   All Rights Reserved

Adding Plants 1 –

Crafting Your Own Plants

A small town devoid of plants would be incomplete. Let's cultivate some greenery.

The brush I use for creating plants is **Realistic Watercolor > Rough wash**. Feel free to experiment with various brushes to achieve different effects. Currently, my plant resembles broccoli. Painting detailed plants with built-in brushes can be time-consuming, so for now, let's explore a quicker method to grow our plants.

Adding Plants 2 –

Using Brushes for Plant Creation

As I mentioned earlier, there's no need to reinvent the wheel each time. In this instance, we can download a variety of brushes as assets to create greenery for our small town. Here is the first brush that I downloaded specifically for the trees lining the sidewalk in front of the buildings (mall):

https://assets.clip-studio.com/en-us/detail?id=1755643

Art by: Grandpa Edo   All Rights Reserved

Once we are satisfied with the shape of this tree, we'll need to adjust the perspective ruler again – it might seem rigid, but it's necessary in this case.

For a clearer view, I recommend deselecting the **Color Folder** (or **Color Layer**, if you're not using a folder to group layers), so you can see the trees in the clean perspective view. Remember the golden rule of perspective – the closer an object is, the larger it appears.

Art by: Grandpa Edo   All Rights Reserved

After re-selecting the Color Folder, we can proceed to erase any unnecessary parts of the trees, ensuring they appear as if they're standing behind the street café.

Art by: Grandpa Edo   All Rights Reserved

Additionally, we'll add some mosses on the surface of the Medieval castle. The brush I used to paint the moss growing on the Medieval Castle is this one:

https://assets.clip-studio.com/en-us/detail?id=1754189

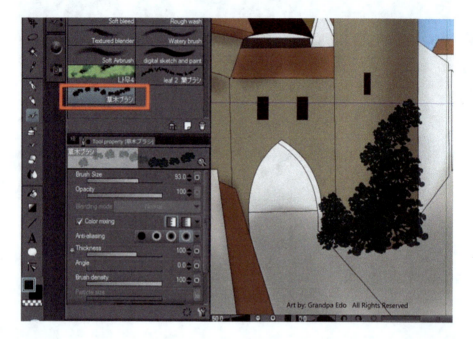

To replace the ''broccoli'' style tree I painted earlier, I downloaded an Image Material, then dragged and dropped it onto the canvas. Here is the link for this Image Material: https://assets.clip-studio.com/en-us/detail?id=1380311

Once again, I adjusted its position and erased any unnecessary parts of the tree to make it look as realistic as the tree growing behind the castle.

Art by: Grandpa Edo   All Rights Reserved

As for the flowers and plants next to the café, I used these two brushes: https://assets.clip-studio.com/en-us/detail?id=1753487

Art by: Grandpa Edo   All Rights Reserved

The Foliage plants: https://assets.clip-studio.com/en-us/detail?id=1734799 and the falling leaves on the café umbrellas: https://assets.clip-studio.com/en-us/detail?id=1756207

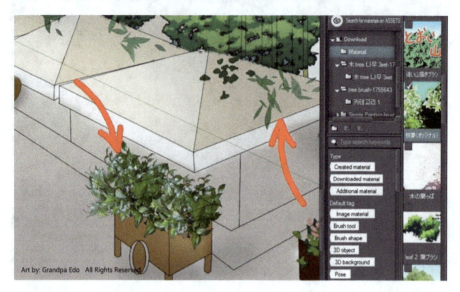

To paint the grasses on the lawn, I used the following brush https://assets.clip-studio.com/en-us/detail?id=1756648. Applying various green colors creates a sense of thickness, topped with yellow highlight for added depth.

Adding Other Small Objects -

Using the 3D Method

We still need a few more details to bring this corner to life. That girl lying next to the grass appears to be someone who loves sports, so let's give her a bicycle. We can download one from our ''Material Library''. Simply navigate to **Window** > **Material** > **Material [Material]** > **3D** > **Small objects**.

Art by: Grandpa Edo   All Rights Reserved

Feel free to experiment with the control handles above the 3D model to achieve your desired result.

To integrate it into the scene, we scale down the bicycle, place it onto the grass, and then add a 3D football. Now, she's a typical sports girl resting there.

So how far have we come? Let's take a look now.

Art by: Grandpa Edo   All Rights Reserved

Ok, so far we have our lead actress, the flying doctor, a supporting actress who is a sports girl, and a colorful small town with a blue sky and greenery. We can now move on to our next stage – You are the director.

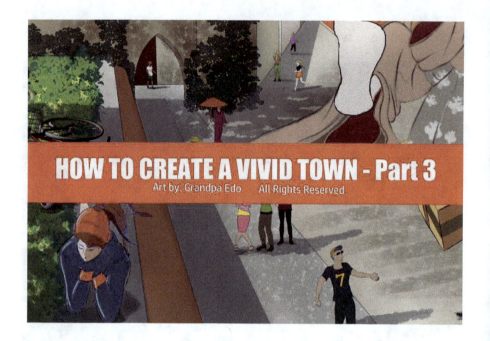

HOW TO CREATE A VIVID TOWN - Part 3
Art by: Grandpa Edo   All Rights Reserved

CHAPTER 3

You Are a Director

Even with correct perspective, an artwork of a small town might still feel dull, lacking the daily hustle and bustle of life. Having played the roles of both Architect and God, we've set up our stage. The next step is to add more Extras. Let's do it now.

Telling a Story through Staging Extras

Remember how we imported our supporting actress (the sports girl) from the 3D Model library? Simply follow the same procedure –

Go to **Window** > **Material** > **Material [Material]** > **3D** > **Pose** > **Entire body**. Then proceed with the usual manipulation, such as fine-tuning the angle of 3D models, and scaling them down to fit into the scene, etc.

But let's not stop there. In ancient Greece, theaters were built in open-air structures on the slope of mountains. So, why not transform this quiet sidewalk into a Street Theater? Group some 3D models together and let them tell a story.

Art by: Grandpa Edo   All Rights Reserved

Art by: Grandpa Edo   All Rights Reserved

Now that we've deployed our extras into this small town, let's once again check the perspective of these characters – Remember, the closer an object is, the larger it appears. We have four different sizes of characters to demonstrate the perspective (see yellow numbers in the image).

1) Largest – the flying doctor

2) Second largest – the sports girl

3) Third largest – most of the extras close to us

4) Smallest – those Extras in the further distance, almost resembling dots

Additionally, note that the position of the sports girl is much higher than those extras on the street, but much lower than the flying doctor in the sky.

Art by: Grandpa Edo   All Rights Reserved

Once we are happy with the general deployment of the extras, we can start refining the details.

Once more, we may need to **erase** any unnecessary parts of these 3D extras to fit them seamlessly into the scene.

Art by: Grandpa Edo   All Rights Reserved

Then, let's have a little fun.

Art by: Grandpa Edo   All Rights Reserved

Art by: Grandpa Edo   All Rights Reserved

Art by: Grandpa Edo   All Rights Reserved

A similar process can be applied to other extras in the scene until we have all our extras dressed up on the street. They might appear tiny in the final scene, but it's these extras that give us a sense of the real world.

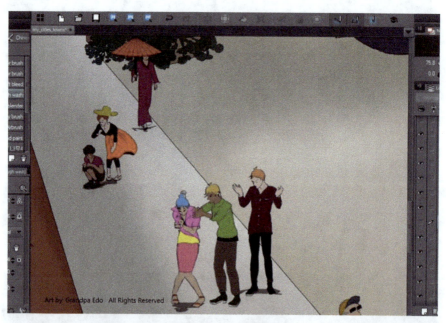

Art by: Grandpa Edo   All Rights Reserved

Art by: Grandpa Edo   All Rights Reserved

Adding Texture to Enhance Realism

Our small town is becoming more lively, but the overall appearance still seems too ''new and clean'', especially for those two Medieval castles. We need to apply some textures to evoke a sense of history. Now, you're also an art director.

I use this brush for the texture of the medieval castle: https://assets.clip-studio.com/en-us/detail?id=1702947 .

If you decrease the Brush Density to around 45 and increase the Scale Ratio to above 200, you'll achieve a very rough texture ideal for either marble or an aged building like an old castle. Certainly, feel free to experiment with those values.

Art by: Grandpa Edo   All Rights Reserved

Additionally, the street appears too pristine; we may add some texture to it using the same brush.

Art by: Grandpa Edo   All Rights Reserved

Incorporating Shadow for Depth

Lastly, we need to paint the shadow. The ancient Greek poet Pindar used to say, 'Man is a dream of a shadow,' so let's not overlook them. In Part 2, we established the basic light/shadow, and now we can refine it.

The shadow on the left side lawn and the shadows of the trees might require extra attention. For this, I used the **Brush** > **Realistic Watercolor** > **Rough Wash**. This brush creates an interesting edge for the shadow. We're almost there! Just one more little thing, we can finalize this piece.

Art by: Grandpa Edo   All Rights Reserved

Including Small Details to Enrich the Scene

The right-side building houses a shopping mall, and nestled around the corner is a quaint café called "Alien Cafe". It's rumored that some extraterrestrial visitors stop by here for a cup of coffee. Since they don't dress like us – well, that's just a convenient excuse for my laziness. Perhaps we can create a signboard for the café, or simply leave it as is.

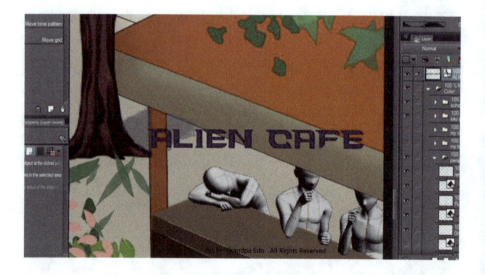

OK, our journey of creating a vivid small town has come to an end. Let's take a final look at this painting with a clockwise view.

Art by: Grandpa Edo All Rights Reserved

Art by: Grandpa Edo All Rights Reserved

Art by: Grandpa Edo   All Rights Reserved

Art by: Grandpa Edo   All Rights Reserved

This is an ordinary day, when a flying doctor from the Edo period accidentally arrives in this small town. She witnesses a slice of life here, and I hope she enjoys our small town. I also hope this creative journey was interesting, inspirational, and helpful.

Thank you for reading! While this marks the end of our mini journey, I hope it will open doors to many creative possibilities in your life. Keep being creative!

Art by: Grandpa Edo   All Rights Reserved

END OF JOURNEY

Exercises and Practices

Exercise 1: Create your ideal place
- Create a simple landscape scene based on your hand-drawn sketch. Pay attention to the perspective.

Exercise 2: Coloring your background
- Use the "masking" technique from Chapter 2 to create a colorful background.
- Use various "brushes" to enhance the appearance of your environment.

Exercise 3: Storytelling
- Use your imagination to create a simple scenario for your place.

Exercise 4: Character design
- Use the technique from Chapter 3 to create your 3D characters. Integrate them into your environment.

Have fun!

Logic will get you from A to Z.
Imagination will get you everywhere.

Albert Einstein

ABOUT THE AUTHOR

 Grandpa Edo is an experienced artist living in Australia. He is also a designer and a writer.

Grandpa Edo believes a storyteller lives in everyone's soul, awakening only when we slow down in real life. During such amazing moments of awakening, we may wander into our soul's garden to visit this storyteller in secret.

Grandpa Edo's mission is simple: to tell interesting stories in various forms, whether through art tutorials, words, or audio.

Apart from doing all these creative works, Grandpa Edo loves cooking, listening to music, walking, and more.

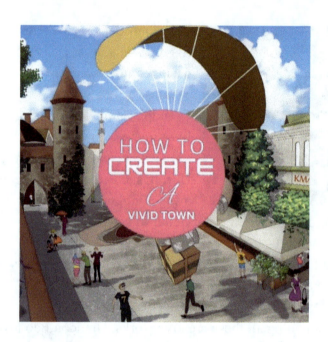

www.ingramcontent.com/pod-product-compliance
Lightning Source LLC
La Vergne TN
LVHW051741050326
832903LV00023B/1039

Grandpa Edo is an experienced artist living in Australia. He is also a designer and a writer.

Grandpa Edo believes a storyteller lives in everyone's soul, awakening only when we slow down in real life. During such amazing moments of awakening, we may wander into our soul's garden to visit this storyteller in secret.

Grandpa Edo's mission is simple: to tell interesting stories in various forms, whether through art tutorials, words, or audio.

Welcome to an inspiring tutorial that guides you through my creative journey and offers essential tips on crafting a vibrant small town. This unique book goes beyond a standard digital painting tutorial, aiming to ignite your imagination and creativity.

While this guide utilizes Clip Studio Paint, the techniques can be applied with other similar software, or you can draw inspiration for your conceptual projects. The creative process is more important than any specific software.

What's Inside:

Chapter 1 – You Are an Architect: Lay the foundations and design your small town with meticulous attention to detail.

Chapter 2 – You Are God: Breathe life into your creation, adding elements that make your town vibrant and dynamic.

Chapter 3 – You Are a Director: Create compelling scenes and bring your vision to life with storytelling techniques.

This step-by-step walkthrough is crafted for artists of all levels, offering practical insights and creative inspiration. Note that the author and artist of this book, Grandpa Edo, is not affiliated with Celsys, the developer of Clip Studio Paint.

Unlock your creativity and start crafting your vibrant small town today!

ISBN 9798329064049

90000

9 798329 064049